PLEADING FOR ISRAEL

TABITHA BLEDSOE

AuthorHouse™
1663 Liberty Drive
Bloomington, IN 47403
www.authorhouse.com
Phone: 1 (800) 839-8640

Published by AuthorHouse 05/31/2018

ISBN: 978-1-5462-4223-9 (sc)
ISBN: 978-1-5462-4222-2 (e)

Library of Congress Control Number: 2018906165

Print information available on the last page.

Scripture quotations marked NIV are taken from the Holy Bible, New International Version®. NIV®. Copyright © 1973,
1978, 1984 by International Bible Society. Used by permission of Zondervan. All rights reserved. [Biblica]

Scripture quotations marked KJV are from the Holy Bible, King James Version (Authorized Version). First published
in 1611. Quoted from the KJV Classic Reference Bible, Copyright © 1983 by The Zondervan Corporation.

This book is printed on acid-free paper.

authorHOUSE®

PLEADING FOR ISRAEL

01

In order to know where you are going you need to know where you came from. Here in America the Negros have been told that they came from Africa, and that their own people sold them into slavery. But, what is our history prior to that? In fact; I will prove that all that was taught to us have been lies, lies, and more lies.

Did you notice that about every five years your nationality changed? You were called Colored people, Blacks, Negros, Afro-American, and now African-American. All of this was done by design, to keep you from finding out who you really are. You were the best kept secret. America has paid trillions of dollars to keep this information from you. And believe it or not it is hidden in books. Now I don't know if you know the saying (proverb) "If you want to hide something from a nigger just put it in a book." Well, this is the saying and is this really true? For us, who really wanted the truth, we began to do the research as the MOST HIGH has lead us to do and this is what I've found.

Hello, as you know my name is Tabitha Bledsoe, and I'm going to share with you my life experiences to show you how I came to this point of my life. I'm the oldest of three children from my mother Barbara Boyd. Both of her parents were Pastors. So, I grew up in the Christian faith. Years later days before I turned five my mother married a Pastor's son. With this union I became Apostolic-Pentecostal. During this time, I knew that I believed in my Jesus. All I wanted to do was tell everyone about him and how he can save their souls. One day my step grandmother seen that I was trying leave the house so she asked me where I was going. I told her that I just wanted to tell everybody about Jesus. She got all excited and told me that I was a special child. She kept reminding me of this until she passed. I didn't think that I was all that special, I just loved my savior and wanted to share with everyone I saw. As I got older I began to have dreams and seeing them come to pass. The dream that really stuck to me was when in about the seventh grade when my friend had lost his brother to brain tumor, months later after the funeral I remember that it was on a Saturday night that I dreamt that I saw his coffin standing up and the coffin opened up I was scared and jumped, but when it opened I saw that it was empty. That Sunday morning, I woke up and told my mother that I dreamt that his body was missing. Neither her or I understood why I had that dream until later that day at church when his mother stood up and testified that her son's body was missing and how upset she was. She then began to tell us that she found out that they took him to do some testing on his body, without her permission. After this I was really amazed.

Well, finding out that I had the gift of sight was amazing to me, but that wasn't all a little later I began to hear his voice, he first started troubling me about keeping the Sabbaths. According to the Bible and all through it we are supposed to keep the Sabbaths, so that was one strike against the Christian Church. I asked people but they all kept telling me that because Jesus died on a Friday and rose on a Sunday that's why we went to church on Sunday. So, I was like ok, but it still bothered me.

After a while he then started troubling me about the so called three days that they tell us he died on a Friday. He told me to count those day so I did and only came up with two. Later, when I came into this truth he showed me in **Daniel 9:27** that he died on a Wednesday and rose at the end of the Sabbath. Jesus (Yahusha) never broke any of the Laws. Yet, the Christians use him to break the Sabbath. And to really tell the truth the Sabbath that they claim to keep many of them really are not keeping that day either. According to the Bible we are not to work, cook, clean, buy, sell, or do any of our pleasures such as marital lovemaking, television, etc. on that day. Scriptures to back that up:

Exodus 31:15 Six days may work be done; but in the seventh is the Sabbath of rest, holy to Yah: whosoever doeth any work in the Sabbath day, he shall surely be put to death.

Nehemiah10: 31 And if the people of the land bring ware or any victuals on the Sabbath day to sell, that we would not buy it of them on the Sabbath, or on the holy day:

Two strikes against Christianity, so I'm really thinking now. Whoa, what is going on? Never the less he began showing me something else. Now, he began telling me that the Bible declares everything from the beginning to the end, right. Then why is it that we don't know who most of the people are that's in the Bible? The only people mainly known are the Hamites? Even though some still get confused and think that the Canaanites are white people. How can that be when Ham is the Proginator of the dark races, not the negroes, but Cush, Mitzraim(Egypt), Phut, and the fourth being Caanan,(Zondervan Compact Dictionary) so who was I and everyone else according to the Bible. This answer I didn't get until I fully came into the truth and started to get the understanding of the Word. To get this understanding he took me to the scriptures in **Psalms:**

Psalms 49:11 Their inward thought is, that their houses shall continue forever, and their dwelling places to all generation; they call their lands after their own names.

Here he showed me that he was speaking about Edom, as they were stealing lands they renamed them after their own names and that's the Identity they became. Therefore, we got some Americans, Itailians,

Africans, etc. Mind you none of these names are in the Bible. The MOST HIGH gave each nation a name and those names still exist as so the people. And with his guidance I now know who the people are according to the Bible. All praises to the MOST HIGH for showing me these truths.

Later in life, about my mid- twenties I started to dream some things that I couldn't interpret at that time. One of the most vivid dream was that I was at this church that I attended, Monument of Hope, in Carbondale, IL., and I was standing on the side while the members were walking to enter the building. At the same time the Pastor, Rev. Morgan and his wife were standing behind me. I was trying to tell the Saints not to enter the church. I remember yelling don't' go in there. No one would listen, but as they were entering the building I noticed that they fell into a trance as if they were sleep walking. I then woke up, confused and wondering why was I telling the people not to go into the church. That was very strange but I remembered this dream for a long time and pondered over it. I still couldn't get the meaning of it.

Years went by and I forgot all about the dream up until March 2015, when I fully woke up and seen the truth. The dream then came back into my mind and then I got the interpretation of the dream. I was in fact trying to tell the members to come out of Christianity and no one would listen. Pretty much that was happening then and still is today. No one wants to research what I'm telling them, so then he put it in me to write this book and show you what he has shown me. I pray that every opens their hearts and minds and be able to see as I have.

Now to get me started on this path which began around February 2000, which was when I had according to men a Nervous breakdown. Unlike some of who I spoke to who don't remember anything that happened during their breakdown I remember pretty much everything. During this time, I was having visions back to back to back. I was having them while I was awake, and while I was asleep. One of the visions I had was as I was watching TBN, Christian Network. I began to see preachers dying going to hell, then I saw my family members who were preachers and deacons and people that I believed to be saved most of their life dying and going to hell. I remember asking why are these people going to Hell? I believed that they were right with the Lord. Then I heard his voice tell me because they didn't know him. I was confused because most of these people I personally knew and they told me and I thought that they actually showed me that they knew him. These like my aunt and uncle I actually seen had a prayer life, and continually stayed in the Word and actually lived what they preached. So, you can imagine my confusion.

I now understand those visions and the Bible, but it took me to follow and do his commandments. The more I did the commandments the more he showed me truths.

Psalms 111:10 The fear of YAH is the beginning of wisdom: a good understanding have all they that do his commandments: his praise endureth forever.

Isaiah 49:5 And now, saith Yah that formed me from the womb to be his servant, too bring Jacob again to him, though Israel be not gathered, yet shall I be glorious in the eyes of Yah, and my Yah shall be my strength.

Isaiah 49:6 And he said, It is a light thing that thou shouldest be my servant to raise up the tribes o Jacob, and to restore the preserved of Israel: I will also give thee for a light to the Gentiles, that thou mayest be my salvation unto the end of the earth.

Deuteronomy chapter 32 verse 26: I said I would scatter them into corners, I would make the remembrance of them to cease among men;

Deuteronomy chapter 32 verse 28: For they are a nation void of counsel, neither is there any understanding in them. Israel (precept for this is in Proverbs 11:14)

Proverbs 11:14 Where no counsel is, the people fall: but in the multitude of counsellors there is safety.

CHAPTER 1 WHO IS ISRAEL?

In those scriptures it tells you that **Israel** will be scattered among the nations. That they won't remember who they are, and the other nations (all people) also won't know who they are. They don't operate together as a nation of people and they have no understanding of what has happening to them, why it is still happening, and what is actually going on around them in this world. Before YAH UAH woke me up I was still in the delusion. Now being woken up I see things more clear and understand the scriptures. What a lot of people don't understand is that the **Bible** is the history book of Israel that also tells the future of all nations.

YAH UAH used nations to scatter the Israelites. Psalms chapter 83 verses 1 through 8 will show you the nations that were involved in the prophecy of Deuteronomy 32:26.

Psalms 83:1 Keep not thou silence, O Yah: hold not thy peace, and be not still, O Yah.

Psalms 83:2 For, lo thine enemies make a tumult: and they that hate thee have lifted up the head.

Psalms 83:3 They have taken crafty counsel against thy people, and consulted against thy hidden ones. (YAH UAH has **hidden them** from the whole word **including themselves (Israel),** no one know who the real **Israel** are**).**

Psalms 83:4 They have said, Come, and let us cut them off from being a nation; that the name of Israel may be no more in remembrance.

Psalms 83:5 For they have consulted together with one consent: they are confederate against thee:

Psalms 83:6 The tabernacles of Edom, and the Ishmaelites; of Moab. And the Hagarenes;

Psalms 83:7 Gebal, and Ammon, and Amelek; the Philistines with the inhabitants of Tyre;

Psalms 83:8 Assur also is joined with them: they have holpen the children of Lot.

Edom today is the so-called white man, I'll show you this from the scriptures, Zondervan Compact Bible Dictionary, and the book of Classical Biblical Names:

Genesis 25:21 And Isaac entreated Yah for his wife, because she was barren: and Yah was entreated of him, and Rebekah his wife conceived.

Genesis 25:22 And the children struggled together within her; and she said, If it be so, why am I thus? And she went to inquire of Yah.

Genesis 25:23 And Yah said unto her, <u>two (2) nations</u> are in thy womb, and two manner of people shall be separated from thy bowels; and the one people shall be stronger than the other people; and the elder shall serve the younger.

Genesis 25:24 And when her days to be delivered were fulfilled, behold, there were twins in her womb.

Genesis25:25 And the first came out red, all over like a hairy garment; and they called his name Esau.

Genesis 25:26 And after that came his brother out, and his hand took hold on Esau's heel; and his name was called Jacob: and Isaac was threescore years old when she bare them.

Now going to the Authorized (King James) Version of the Apocrypha:

II Esdras 6:8 And he said unto me, From Abraham unto Isaac, when Jacob and Esau were born of him, Jacob's hand held first the heel of Esau.

II Esdras 6:9 For Esau is the end of the world, and Jacob is the beginning of it that followeth.

With that, who is ruling the world today? Yes, most of us know that right now it is the white man's world. But to give you more proof that Esau is the so called white man the bible also gives you their characteristics:

Genesis 25:27 And the boys grew: and Esau was a cunning hunter, a man of the field;

Genesis 25:30 And Esau said unto Jacob, feed me, I pray thee, with that same red pottage; for I am faint.

In those scriptures it shows you that Esau came out red and hairy all over. Now most people know that

White people are not white. They are not the color of the white paper. They are red or pinkish in color because the blood shows through their skin. Second it shows that they are hunters, people of the field. To this day they are still hunters. Third it shows that they like to eat their food with blood. Still to this day many of them still like their food this way.

For those that still don't believe that Edom is the race of the so called white man. I have the Zondervan Compact Bible Dictionary completed by your Christian Scholars.

Edom, Edomites (red), the nation and its people who were the descendants of Esau. He founded the country, so his name is equated with Edom (Gen. 25:30 36:1,8). The country was also called Seir, which was the name of the territory in which the Edomites lived.

Now, I'm going to the last paragraph of Edom's definition because it is fairly long.

Edom figures prominently in the prophetic Scriptures as the scene of great future judgments (see notably Isa. 34:5, 6; 63:1). She is the only neighbor of the Israelites who was not given any promise of mercy from God. (Zondervan Compact Bible Dictionary).

Ishmaelites, this is a Nation that I know many know, but in case you don't these are the Arabs today.

The Moabs are the Chinese today.

The Ammonites are the Japanese today.

The Hagarenes, Tyre, Zidon, and the Philistines are the Africans.

Ammelek is the so called Jewish people today.

This scripture also is about who participated in the Atlantic Slave Trade. What people don't understand is that this scripture also lets you know that these other Nations were and still are God's Enemies. Throughout the Bible you will begin to see. You cannot hate God's people and Love God. Does that make any sense?

Now I'm going to give you the precept to Psalms 83 in Jeremiah 33:24;

Jeremiah 33:24 Considerest thou not what this people have spoken, saying, the two families which Yah hath chosen, (Israel and Judah) he hath even cast them off? Thus they have despised my people, that they should be no more a Nation before them.

In order to find Israel today you need to go to Deuteronomy 28:15-68 these tell you the curses that will be on these people forever. The scripture that tells you this in Deuteronomy 28:46 <u>And</u> <u>they</u> <u>shall</u> <u>be</u> <u>upon</u> <u>thee</u> <u>for</u> <u>a</u> <u>sign</u> <u>and</u> <u>for</u> <u>a</u> <u>wonder,</u> <u>and</u> <u>upon</u> <u>thy</u> <u>seed</u> <u>forever</u>. So, tell me why the Christians are lying telling the people that God has uplifted the curses off Israel and brought them back to their Land? That is not Bible. But it is Bible that shows us who those people really are that are in our land right now. I'll get to that a little later.

In fact, the Bible tells us that the one most people call Jesus (Yahusha) will be gathering Israel himself with his army of the Angels and every eye shall see it. It also lets you know what the people are going to be saying when this happen. This is in the "Wisdom of Solomon" in the Apocrypha Authorized (King James) Version, Chapter 4 and 5.

Wisdom of Solomon 4:14 For his soul pleased the Lord: therefor hasted he to take him away from among the wicked.

Wisdom of Solomon 4:15 This the people saw, and understood it not, neither laid they up this in their minds, that his grace and mercy is with the Saints (Israel), and that he hath respect unto his chosen.

Wisdom of Solomon 4:16 Thus the righteous that is dead shall condemn the ungodly which are living; and youth that is soon perfected the many years and old age of the unrighteous (the truth coming out after many years of non- truth, therefore being made perfect in his truth in a short time.)

Wisdom of Solomon 4:17 For they shall see the end of the wise (Edom), and shall not understand what God in his council hath decreed of him, and to what end the Lord hath set him in safety. (From affliction from all other nations of people.**)**

Wisdom of Solomon 4:18 They shall see him, and despise him; but God shall laugh them to be a vile carcass, and a reproach among the dead for evermore. (All those that hate **Israel**).

Wisdom of Solomon 5:1 Then shall the righteous man stand in great boldness before the face of such has afflicted them, and made no account of his labors. (They murder him and found their selves not guilty.

{**Zechariah 11:5 Whose possessors slay them and hold themselves not guilty: and they that sell them say, Blessed be Yah; for I am rich: and their own shepherds pity them not**} innocent men and women sent to prison, kept them from jobs and **Slavery** (no account of his work). There are more afflictions but I just named a few.

Wisdom of Solomon 5:2 When they see it, they shall be troubled with terrible fear, and shall be amazed at the strangeness of his salvation, so far beyond all they looked for. This is letting you know that **Jesus** the so called **"Rapture"** that the Christians are teaching that people of all races that believe in Christ will be invisibly caught up with no one seeing who took them is a Lie from the pit of Hell.

Wisdom of Solomon 5:3 And they repenting and groaning for anguish of spirit shall say within themselves, this was he, whom we had whom we had sometimes in derision, and a proverb of reproach:

Wisdom of Solomon 5:4 We Fools accounted his life madness, and his end to be without honor:

Wisdom of Solomon 5:5 How is he numbered among the children of God, and his lot is among the saints! (Shows you here that they thought these people to be nothing, kind of like what the nations think of us as a people.)

Wisdom of Solomon 5:6 Therefore have we erred from the way of truth, and the light of righteousness hath not shined unto us, and the sun of righteousness rose not upon us.

Wisdom of Solomon 5:7 We wearied ourselves in the way of wickedness and destruction: yea, we have gone through deserts, where there lay no way: but as for the way of the Lord, we have not known it. (Now, don't this sound like the "Christians" to you? It does to me. This scripture and other precepts with Micah.)

Micah 4:10 Be in pain, and labor to bring forth, (tell your people this truth) **O daughter of Zion, like a woman in travail: for now thou shalt go forth out of the city, and thou shalt dwell in the field, and thou shalt go even to Babylon;** (America) **there shalt thou be delivered; there Yah shall redeem thee from the hand of thine enemies.**

Micah 4:11 Now also many nations are gathered against thee, that say, let her be defiled, and let our eye look upon Zion. (Slavery, and Babylon's world system.)

Micah 4:12 But they know not the thoughts of Yah (God), neither understand they his council: for he shall gather them as Slavery the sheaves into the floor.j

Micah 4:13 Arise and thresh, O daughter of Zion: for I will make thine horn iron, and I will make thy hoofs brass: and thou shalt beat in pieces many people: and I will consecrate their gain unto Yah (God), and their substance unto the ALL MIGHTY of the whole earth.

Now, most the scriptures that I have given you shows you that Israel is hated by all the other Nations, so who is Israel? I'm going to show you who they are according to Deuteronomy 28:15-68. If you remembered the story of Moses and his people (Israel), that Yah (God) led them out of Egypt (Bondage). In the wilderness Yah gave them his laws and statutes that they were to live by forever. There they entered into a blood covenant with YAH UAH. (God) Which the Bible is divided into two Covenants. (Testaments) people all over tried to take the new Covenant for their selves using John 3:16, but have no understanding that Yah (God) has not and, was not dealing with any other nation. He tells us this over and over in the scriptures, and I'll show you later on. The first covenant they had to keep the laws and statutes, and the Law of sacrifice for their sins. The second covenant they still had to keep the laws and statutes, but the Law of sacrifice was done away with by the blood of Yahusha (Jesus), therefore giving us grace and mercy (time to get it right) instead of dying as soon as we commit those sins as in the old days. Christ told us this in the scriptures. And what a lot of people don't know is that there will also be a new covenant after he gathers Israel and bring them back into their land. I'll show this to you also.

Let's, find out who are the Hebrew Israelites according to the scriptures. According to these curses you shall find Israel in the last days.

Deuteronomy 28: 15 But it shall come to pass, if thou wilt not hearken unto the voice of YAH UAH thy ALL MIGHTY, which I command thee this day, to observe to do all his commandments and his statutes which I command thee this day; that all these curses shall come upon thee, and overtake thee:

Deuteronomy 28:16 Cursed shalt thou be in the city, and cursed shalt thou be in the field.

(Wherever you go you will be cursed).

Deuteronomy 28:17 Cursed shall be thy basket and thy store.(we will get the worst foods in our neighborhood.)

Deuteronomy 28:18 Cursed shall be the fruit of thy body, and the fruit of thy land, the increase of thy kine, and the flocks of thy sheep.

Deuteronomy 28:19 Cursed shalt thou be when thou comest in, and cursed shalt thou be when thou goest out.

Deuteronomy 28:20 Yah shall send upon thee cursing, vexation, and rebuke, in all that thou settest thine hand unto for to do, until thou be destroyed, and until thou perish quickly; because of the wickedness of thy doings, whereby thou hast forsaken me.

Deuteronomy 28:21 Yah shall make the pestilence cleave unto thee, (bugs, mice, rats) until he have consumed thee from off the land, whither thou goest to possess it. (Will follow you wherever you live.)

Deuteronomy 28:22 Yah shall smite thee with consumption, and with fever, and with an inflammation, and with extreme burning, and with the sword, and with blasting, and with mildew; and they shall pursue thee until thou be destroyed.

Deuteronomy 28: 23 And thy heaven that is over thy head shall be brass, and the earth that is under thee shall be iron. (This is the prison, and jail)

Deuteronomy 28:24 Yah shall make the rain of thy land powder and dust: from heaven shall it come down upon thee, until thou be destroyed.

Deuteronomy 28:25 Yah shall cause thee to be smitten before thine enemies: thou shalt go out one way against them, and flee seven ways before them: and shalt be removed into all the kingdoms of the earth. (Won't be victorious any more, and won't have your own land).

Deuteronomy 28: 26 And thy carcass shall be meat unto the fowls of the air, and unto beasts of the earth, and no man shall fray them away. (You'll die in the streets, trees, and animals such as lions, dogs attack you at command.) This has been happening for centuries.

Deuteronomy 28: 27 Yah will smite thee with the botch of Egypt, and with the emerods, and with the scab, and with the itch, whereof thou canst not be healed.

Deuteronomy 28: 28 Yah shall smite thee with madness, and blindness, and astonishment of heart:

Deuteronomy 28:29 And thou shalt grope at noonday, as the blind grope in darkness, and thou shalt not prosper in thy ways: and thou shalt be only oppressed and spoiled evermore, and no man shall save thee. (You'll never get out of these conditions as a nation, Malcom X couldn't save you, Martin Luther King couldn't save you, your Pastors couldn't save you, plus they won't give you reparations like they did the other nations. The only one that is going to save us is **YAH UHA, through his son YAH USHA**. This bible is real and true!!! **YAH UAH THY ALMIGHTY** made it so that **EDOM** got up so high that only he can save us. Just like in **EGYPT** with the **PHAROH**.

Deuteronomy 28:30 Thou shalt betroth a wife, and another man shall lie with her: thou shalt build a house, and thou shalt not dwell therein: thou shalt plant a vineyard, and shalt not gather the grapes thereof. (All of this happened in slavery).

Deuteronomy 28:31 Thine ox shall be slain before thine eyes, and thou shalt not eat thereof:

Thine ass shall be violently taken away from before thy face, and shall not be restored to thee: thy sheep shall be given unto thine enemies, and thou shalt have none to rescue them. (This happened in 70 A.D. the fall of Judah, Levi, and Benjamin).

Deuteronomy 28:32 Thy sons and thy daughters shall be given to another people, and thine eyes shall look, and fail with longing for them all the day long: and there shall be no might in thine hand. (This also happened in slavery, and still to this day. You will not have the power to do anything about it. No Military force, etc.)

Deuteronomy 28:33 The fruit of thy land, and all thy labors, shall a nation which thou knowest not eat up; and thou shalt be only oppressed and crushed always: (You won't be in your land, another nation will be in your land eating up your fruits, etc. **You are not coming out of this oppression until the end of this time.**) This began in 70 A.D and is still happening today.

Deuteronomy 28:34 So that thou shalt be mad for the sight of thine of thine eyes which thou shalt see. (This began in 70 A.D and is still happening today. Are we not mad when our people get killed by the police, when they plant evidence to lock you up, lose your job for no reason, there's many more.)

Deuteronomy 28:35 Yah shall smite thee in the knees, and in the legs, with a sore botch that cannot be healed, from the sole of thy foot unto the top of thy head.

Deuteronomy 28:36 Yah shall bring thee, and thy kings which thou shalt set over thee, unto a nation which neither thou nor thy fathers have known; and there shalt thou serve other gods, wood and stone. (You are going into slavery in a land faraway, and there you will serve other god's the **WOOD** is **CHRISTIANITY,** the **STONE** is **MUSLIM.)**

Deuteronomy 28:37 And thou shalt become an astonishment, a proverb, and a byword, among all nations whither Yah shall lead thee. (Negro, Colored, black, Moore, coon, nigger, etc. This is still happening.)

Deuteronomy 28:38 Thou shalt carry much seed out into the field, and shalt gather but little in; for the locust shall consume it. (This still happens today.)

Deuteronomy 28:39 Thou shalt plant vineyards, and dress them, but shalt neither drink of the wine, for the locust shall consume it.

Deuteronomy 28:40 Thou shalt have olive trees throughout all thy coasts, but shalt neither drink of the wine, nor gather the grapes; for the worms shall eat them.

Deuteronomy 28:41 Thou shalt beget sons and daughters, but thou shalt not enjoy them; for they shall go into captivity. (Happened in slavery)

Deuteronomy 28:42 All thy trees and fruit of thy land shall the locust consume.

Deuteronomy 28:43 The stranger that is within thee shall get up above thee very high; and thou shalt come down very low. (Notice, China, Japan, India, Iraq people all came over to the U.S. every one of them are higher than us. They have more business, including your business. Still happening to this day.**)**

Deuteronomy 28:44 He shall lend to thee, and thou shalt not lend to him: he shall be the head, and thou shalt be the tail. (You as a people won't own banks, you'll have to borrow from the other Nations. All other nations will be above you and you will be at a low state forever. Have you ever wondered why we have never gotten up from our condition as a nation? Why do our people continuing to suffer?

Deuteronomy 28:45 Moreover all these curses shall come upon thee, and shall pursue thee, and overtake thee, till thou be destroyed; because thou hearkenedst not unto the voice of YAH UAH thy ALL MIGHTY, to keep his commandments and his statutes which he commanded thee:

Deuteronomy 28:46 AND THEY SHALL BE UPON THEE FOR A SIGN AND FOR A WONDER, AND UPON THY SEED FOR EVER. (Hum, this should explain itself. Sorry, Fred Hammond, we are not Blessed. Neither will we be Blessed until we keep his Laws, and Statutes.)

Deuteronomy 28:47 Because thou servedst not YAH UAH thy ALL MIGHTY with joyfulness, and with gladness of heart, for the abundance of all things;

Deuteronomy 28:48 Therefore shalt thou serve thine enemies which the ALL MIGHTY YAH UAH shall send against thee, in hunger, and in thirst, and in nakedness, and in want of all things: and he shall put a yoke upon thy neck, until he have destroyed thee. (If you want food you have to go to your enemies, water you have to pay your water bill, clothing you have to go to your enemies, and all things like Education, birth, death, homes, you have to go to your enemies. The yoke came off our necks after we were destroyed, not knowing who we were; they took away our culture, names and language from us. **The chains didn't come off our necks meaning physical slavery, didn't end until we were destroyed as a nation. We don't know who we are and have nothing of our culture and heritage as it was fortold by all of the prophets, including Moses.**)

Deuteronomy 28:49 Yah shall bring a nation against thee from far, from the end of the earth, as swift as the eagle flieth; a nation whose tongue thou shalt not understand;(this lets you know that the nation of Edom will get you and you will not understand their language. I know the nation is Edom because the Bible uses the eagle many times for them**.)**

Deuteronomy 28:50 A nation of fierce countenance, which shall not regard the person of the old, nor show favor to the young: (This happened in slavery, alligator babies, lynching the old and the young, and still happens to this day. Police killings young and old**.)**

Deuteronomy 28:51 And he shall eat the fruit of thy cattle, and the of thy land, until thou be destroyed: which also shall not leave thee either corn, wine, or oil, or the increase of thy kine, or flocks of thy sheep, until he have destroyed thee.

Deuteronomy 28:52 And he shall besiege thee in all thy gates, until thy high and fenced walls come down, wherein thou trusted, throughout all thy land: and he shall besiege thee in all thy gates throughout all thy land, which YAH UAH thy ALL MIGHTY hath given thee. (Happened in 70 A.D.)

Deuteronomy 28:53 And thou shalt eat the fruit of thine own body, the flesh of thy sons and of thy daughters, which YAH UAH thy ALL MIGHTY hath given thee, in the siege, and in the straightness, wherewith thine enemies shall distress thee: (this happened in the siege of 70 A.D.)

Deuteronomy 28:54 So that the man that is tender among you, and very delicate, his eye shall be evil toward his brother, and toward the wife of his bosom, and toward the remnant of his children whom he shall eat. (Happened 70 A.D. and still to this day our people don't get along, men hating on the women of our nation, and fatherless homes.)

Deuteronomy 28:55 So that he will not give to any of them of the flesh of his children whom he shall eat: because he hath nothing left him in the siege, and in the straightness, wherewith thine enemies shall distress thee:

Deuteronomy 28:56 The tender and delicate woman among you, which would not adventure to set the sole of her foot upon the ground for delicateness and tenderness, her eye shall be evil toward the husband of her bosom, and toward her son, and toward her daughter, (Happened in 70 A.D. and still to this day)

Deuteronomy 28:57 And toward her young one that cometh out from between her feet, and toward her children which she shall bear: for she shall eat them for want of all things secretly in the siege and straightness, wherewith thine enemy shall distress thee in thy gates.

Deuteronomy 28:58 If thou wilt not observe to do all the words of this law that are written in this book, that thou mayest fear this glorious and fearful name, YAH UAH THY ALLMIGHTY;

Deuteronomy 28:59 Then Yah will make thy plagues wonderful, and the plagues of thy seed, even great plagues of thy seed, even great plagues, and of long continuance, and sore sickness, and of long continuance.

Deuteronomy 28:60 Moreover he will bring upon thee all the diseases of Egypt, which thou wast afraid of; and they shall cleave unto thee.

Deuteronomy 28:61 Also every sickness, and every plague, which is not written in the book of this law, them will Yah bring upon thee, until thou be destroyed. (Still happening)

Deuteronomy 28:62 And ye shall be left few in number, whereas ye were as the stars of heaven for multitude; because thou wouldest not obey the voice of YAH UAH thy ALL MIGHTY. (Still to this day, we are separated in small numbers all over and don't have a land of our own that we would be as the number of the stars as we once were before our sins.)

Deuteronomy 28:63 And it shall come to pass, that as Yah rejoiced over you to do good, and to multiply you; so Yah will rejoice over you to destroy you, and to bring you to nought; and ye shall be plucked from off the land whither thou goest to possess it.

Deuteronomy 28:64 And Yah shall scatter thee among all people, from the one end of the earth even unto the other; and there thou shalt serve other gods, which neither thou nor thy fathers have known, even wood and stone. (You will be scattered among all nations, not having your own land, and there you shall serve **other gods, and he's telling you again** wood(**Christianity**) and stone (**Muslim**). Believe it or not the **Bible** is against religion and I will show you this later.

Deuteronomy 28:65 And among these nations shalt thou find no ease, neither shall the sole of thy feet have rest: but Yah shall give thee there a trembling heart, and failing eyes, and sorrow of mind: (This was really bad during slavery and after slavery ended; the murders of our people by lynchings, bombs (Black Wall Street, Red Summer riots), the KKK attacking your homes and churches, and still today white kid goes into a church and murder black people, and let's not forget about the police killings that just keep happening.)

Deuteronomy 28:66 And thy life shall hang in doubt before thee: and thou shalt fear day and night, and shalt have none assurance of thy life:

Deuteronomy 28:67 In the morning thou shalt say, Would Yah it were even! And at even thou shalt say, Would Yah it were morning! For the fear of thine heart wherewith thou shalt fear, and for the sight of thine eyes which thou shalt see.

Deuteronomy 28:68 And Yah shall bring thee into EGYPT (BONDAGE) again with SHIPS, by the way whereof I spake unto thee, Thou shalt see it no more again: and there ye shall be sold unto your enemies for bondmen (slave men), and bondwomen (slave women), and no man shall buy you.

If this don't get your attention nothing will. Our people are the only people that went into slavery on slave ships. The Trans-Atlantic Slave Trade. Then it tells us that we won't see our homeland again, and no man will help us get out of this one. Think about it we've been marching for years and still going through the same thing, singing WE SHALL OVER COME, now it's BLACK LIVES MATTER. Now the reason for this scripture being last is because this is prophecy of the last captivity. When this captivity is over we will be going home and contrary to your Christian belief every eye shall see it. This is the second Exodus which is also in scripture.

Everything that I'm telling you I'm going to back up with scripture as the Most High has shown unto me. Now to show you that every eye shall see the 2nd Exodus I'm going to go to the book of The Wisdom of Solomon, in the Apocrypha.

Wisdom of Solomon 4: 15 This the people, and understood it not, neither laid they up this in their minds, that his grace and mercy is with his saints, (Israel) and that he hath respect unto his chosen.

Wisdom of Solomon 4:16 Thus the righteous that is dead shall condemn the ungodly which are living; and youth that is soon perfected the many years and old age of the unrighteous.

Wisdom of Solomon 4:17 For they shall see the end of the wise, (Israel) and shall not understand what God in his counsel hath decreed of him in safety.

Wisdom of Solomon 4:18 They shall see him, and despise him; but GOD shall laugh them to scorn: and they shall hereafter be a vile carcass, and a reproach among the dead for evermore.

Wisdom of Solomon 5:1 Then shall a righteous man stand in great boldness before the face of such as have afflicted him, and made no account of his labors. (Those that oppressed him, and made him a slave.)

Wisdom of Solomon 5:2 When they see it, they shall be troubled with terrible fear, and shall be amazed at the strangeness of his salvation, so far beyond all they looked for. (No secret **Rapture,** every eye shall see him.)

Wisdom of Solomon 5:3 And they repenting and groaning for anguish of spirit shall say within themselves, this was he, whom we had sometimes in derision, and a proverb of reproach: (Deuteronomy 28: 37 And thou shalt become an astonishment, a proverb, and a by word, among all nations whither YAH shall lead thee,)

Wisdom of Solomon 5:4 We fools accounted his life madness, and his end to be without honor:

Wisdom of Solomon 5:5 How is he numbered among the children of God, and his lot among the saints!

Wisdom of Solomon 5:6 Therefore have we erred from the way of the truth, and the light of

Wisdom of Solomon 5:7 We wearied ourselves in the way of wickedness and destruction: yea, we have gone through desserts, where there lay no way: but as for the way of the Lord, we have not known it.

In those scriptures it shows you that everyone will see who's the real chosen people are and they are not going to like who they are. Coming into this truth I've seen that many other nations (races) do don't like or believe that we the American Negroes, Hispanics, Haitians, Jamaicans, etc. are the chosen people. Even though the Bible proves it over, and over again. As a matter of fact, the **MOST HIGH** himself is telling people in all of these Nations including my family that we are Israel, and he backed it up with the proofs through scripture and showing us other things. Like we came across some knowledge that in fact there was an archeologist that did some studies on the slaves that were in America. He compared skulls of the so called African-American slaves with some of the Hamites (so called Africans) skulls and said that these we not the same people. Then he compared them with the Israelites that did servitude in Egypt and discovered that these were the same people. There is a scripture that proves this in Revelations.

Revelations 12:16 And the earth helped the woman, (Israel) and the earth opened her mouth, and swallowed up the flood which the dragon cast of his mouth. (This scripture lets you know that there are somethings hidden in the earth that will help you to wake up when the time comes and this prophecy has already come to pass, and still is.)

The whole reason for Israel being in slavery is because we did not obey YAH UAH THE ALMIGHTY!!! We did not keep his Laws, Statutes, and Commandments. Still to this day we are not keeping them. Most of us are following the traditions of men. Meaning religions such as the Bible tells you Wood(Christianity) and Stone(Muslim). The scripture to prove this is in Isaiah.

Isaiah 29:13 Wherefore Yah(God) said, for as much as this people draw near me with their mouth, and with their lips do honor me, but have removed their heart(mind) far from me, and their fear toward me is taught by precept of men: (You learned about God through your manmade religions and you still follow man's traditions, not studying and researching for yourself.)

Luke 6:39 And he spake a parable unto them, Can the blind lead the blind? Shall they not both fall into the ditch?

Luke 6:40 The disciple is not above his master: but every one that is perfect shall be as his master(Lord).

Luke 6:46 And why ye call me Master(Lord), Master(Lord), and do not the things I say? (You do not follow the words of this Bible. All through the Bible it tells **yo**u to keep his commandments all of them and there are more than the 10 commandments, For, instance the dietary laws in Leviticus. One particular in the book of **Leviticus:**

Leviticus 11:7 And the swine, though he divide the hoof, and be clovenfooted, yet he cheweth not the cud, but divideth not the hoof; he is unclean unto you.

Leviticus 11:8 Of their flesh shall ye not eat, and their carcase shall ye not touch: they are unclean to you. (But for some reason all the **Christians** believe that YAH(God) changed his laws because of one scripture of Paul's writings. In which Peter tells you that Paul's writings are hard to understand any many will be destroyed because of the misunderstanding. In that scripture that I'm referring to if you read further you will get the understanding of who and what that scripture was referring to. It was referring to Cornelius, a Jew who became an unclean Gentile, through slavery as we today have become. He had the Law in his heart and was keeping the Law and needed to learn of the Messiah that reconciled (grafted) him back to the Father. It was not talking about eating unclean food.) I have a scripture that confirms what will happen to all those who disobeys the dietary laws in **Isaiah:**

Isaiah 66:15 For, behold, YAH will come with fire, and with his chariots like a whirlwind, to render his anger with fury, and his rebuke with flames of fire.

Isaiah 66: 16 For by fire and by his sword will YAH plead with all flesh: and the slain of YAH shall be many.

Isaiah 66 :17 They that sanctify themselves, and purify themselves in the gardens behind one tree in the midst, eating swine's flesh, and the abomination, and the mouse, shall be consumed together, saith YAH. (This tells you that when he does come back he's going to kill all those who eat things that he told you not to eat. Oh, oh. I've uncovered another lie that CHRISTIANITY has taught us.)

The reason why the people which have awaken to their true Identities, and began to study the word, and do as it told us to do have gotten a better understanding of the Word is because we are doing his will as he commanded us to do. Scripture to back that up is in **Psalms:**

Psalms 111:10 The fear of YAH (God) is the beginning of wisdom: a good understanding have all they that do his commandments: his praise endureth forever.

John 1: 14 And the Word was made flesh, and dwelt among us, (and we beheld his glory, the glory as of the only begotten (of the Father,) full of grace and truth. {He came to show us the way that we ought to walk in. He kept the laws this is the truth and he is the light. The only law that was nailed to the cross is the Law of Sacrifice, and there's where grace comes in, he gave us time to hear the true word and do as the word say. Those who believe in Yah usha will receive the power of the Ruac (Holy Spirit), to have strength to keep YAH Laws. For most Christians I know, know this scripture: **I can do all things through Christ which strengthen me.** The Ruac (Holy Spirit can and will give you the strength to do the laws if you would only return back to the Father and obey him.}

John 4:21 Yah shua saith unto her, Woman, believe me, the hour cometh, when ye shall neither in this mountain, nor yet at Yahrushalom(Jerusalem), worship the Father. (The land will be desolate. As it is now.)

John 4:22 Ye worship ye know not what: we know what we worship: for salvation is of the Jews. (If you are not worshipping how the Bible tells you to worship him than you are not worshipping him in Spirit and in Truth. And salvation is only for Israel.) Everyone in Christianity, including myself missed that. More scriptures to show you that only Israel shall be saved **Romans:**

Romans 9:3 For I Wish that I myself were accursed from Messiah for my brethren, my kinsmen according to the flesh:

Romans 9:4 Who are Israelites; to whom pertaineth the adoption, and the glory, and the covenants, and the giving of the law, and the service of Yah, and the promises;

Romans 9:5 Whose are the fathers, and of whom as concerning the flesh Messiah came, who is over all, YAH blessed forever. YahMain ("So Be It")`1

Now the scriptures tell you what is Spirit and what is truth. Many people believe that if you confess your sins, quote John 3: 16, and believe in Yah shua (Jesus) with all of your heart that you're going to make it to the new kingdom. But, according to the scripture, precept, by precept, line by line, here a little, and there a little. The puzzle then come to you in a better light. There is no hidden meaning in the scriptures. The Bible itself tells you the meaning. More proof of this is in **Isaiah**:

Isaiah 28:13 But the word of YAH was unto them precept upon precept, precept upon precept; line upon line, line upon line; here a little, and there a little;

Now I know this is the time of truth because of these scriptures in Baruch.

Baruch 2:30 For I knew that they would not hear me, because it is a stiff necked people: but in the land of their captivities they shall remember themselves,

Baruch 2:32 And they shall praise me in the land of their captivity, and think upon my name,

Baruch 2:33 And return from their stiff neck, and from their wicked deeds: for they shall remember the way of their fathers, which sinned before the Lord.

Baruch 2:34 And I will bring them again into the land which I promised with an oath unto their fathers, Abraham, Isaac, and Jacob, and they shall be lords of it: and I WILL INCREASE THEM, AND THEY SHAL NOT BE DIMINISHED.

Baruch 2:35 And I will make an everlasting covenant with them to be their God, and they shall be my people: and I will no more drive my people of Israel out of the land that I have given them.

Baruch 2:33-34 is a prophecy being fulfilled today. Many of the Blacks, and Hispanics are waking up to the truth to who they really are according to the Bible, and realizing that they have been lied to. Now many of us are returning to the ways of our fathers that YAH UAH commanded us to do by Moses. This is the only way our people will rise. But, as long as we keep disobeying YAH UAH and his word we will keep dying in the streets, going to prison, being hungry, as well as the other curses of Deuteronomy 28.

What most people don't understand is that **YAH UAH THY ALMIGHTY** do things in order. Do you Know the **MOST HIGH'S** pattern? Well, if you look in the Bible you will see the chapter of Judges. Here he was building Israel and making them strong to fight their enemies, and take their land. Like today, he is rebuilding Israel back up. Doing this he raised up the Judges. Today he's doing the same. He has raised up the Judges to rebuild Israel. These are those camps, and the people on line giving you the scriptures to show you who you are according to the Bible. With this he is bringing back the heart of the father back to the children and the hearts of the children back to the father. This is the spirit of Elisha working now through the Judges. All of this is prophecy that is written in the Bible.

Malachi 4:5 Behold, I will send you Elijah the prophet before the coming of the great and dreadful day of Yah:

Malachi 4:6 And he shall turn the heart of the fathers to the children, and the heart of the children to their fathers, lest I come and smite the earth with a curse.

The Most High will save the tribe of Judah first by waking them up and telling them who they are and showing them who the rest of the tribes are according to the bible. This scripture is in **Zechariah, and Deuteronomy.**

Zechariah 12:7 Yah also shall save the tents of Yahudah(Judah) first, that the glory of the house of David and the glory of the inhabitants of Yahrushalom do not magnify themselves against Yahudah.

Deuteronomy 33:7 And this is the blessing of Yahudah: and he said, hear, ALL MIGHTY YAH UAH, the voice of Yahudah, and bring him unto his people: let his hands be sufficient for him; and be thou an help to him from his enemies.

In those scriptures they tell you that Yahudah will be the first to find out who they are according to the scriptures, and then who will find the other tribes also according to the scriptures. Genesis also prophecies where all the tribes would end in the last days. Meaning this day and time.

The rulers of Edom knew that Yahudah(Judah) would awaken first. This is the main reason for your heavy oppression. You were born into a heavy spiritual warfare and didn't even know it. Many still don't know who you are warring with.

The Elite have been poisoning and plotting to kill you ever since they came into power. Many of us don't even have a clue.

Luke 4:18 The spirit of Yah is upon me, because he hath anointed me to preach the gospel to the poor; he hath sent me to heal the brokenhearted, to preach deliverance to the captives, and recovering of sight to the blind, to set at liberty them that are bruised.

The poor being a nation who doesn't know who they are, and have lost their heritage. The brokenhearted is a nation, which suffer injustices, and have no peace of mind. The captives are the nation that went into slavery and their slavery has not ended yet. I will show proof of this. One scripture proving this is in Deuteronomy.

CHAPTER 2 SLAVERY
STILL EXISTS

Deuteronomy 28:68 And Yah shall bring thee into Egypt again with ships, by the way whereof I spake unto thee, Thou shalt see it no more again (your homeland): and there ye shall be sold unto your enemies for bondmen and bondwomen, an No Man Shall Buy You.

When he said that no man shall buy you, he's letting us know that no one will get us out of our conditions. Including the slavery that he sent us into. I hadn't realized this before, until he had me doing the research. The more I began to dig the more I began to realize that our slavery hasn't ended after all.

Many people were told that Slavery ended with the Civil War and the Emancipation Act. Wrong!!! We have all been lied to.

Deuteronomy 33:29 Happy art thou, O Israel: who is like unto thee, O people saved by Yah, the shield of thy help, and who is the sword of excellency! And thine enemies shall be found liars unto thee; and thou shalt tread upon their high places.

The Bible is the only true book. It is the only book that declares the beginning up until the end. Now, as the scriptures told us the Israel will still be in their slavery when Christ comes back to pick his people up and return them back to their land.

To show me that our slavery hasn't ended, the Most high led me to two books and a video on Netflix.

1. **Slavery by Another Name by Douglas A. Blackmon**
2. **The New Jim Crow by Michelle Douglas**
3. **13ᵗʰ (Video on Netflix)**

Slavery by Another Name was searched out by Douglas because he stumbled on unmarked mass graves of the so-called African-Americans. Before I get started of the horrible truth of the still existing slavery I'm going to ask you if you are aware that according to the United States Constitution the Blacks are still only considered as 3/5 human. Meaning, you still are not considered human. Therefore, you really don't have any rights. In this finding I realized that we are not citizens, but denizens.

Denizen: A foreigner allowed certain rights in the adopted country.

"But, I'm free to come and go as I please." Or "I'm not getting flogged, and forced to work." I know most of the statements that you will come up with to prove that you are free. Yes, you get paid to work. What you and I didn't know is that while the Hebrews were in slavery in the first Egypt(Mitzriam), the Israelites were also in a sense of freedom. When they got done working they went back home. Just as we do today with a false sense of freedom.

On March 30, 1908, a black man was arrested by the sheriff of Shelby County, Alabama. He was charged with a made-up crime just as they do today. This made-up crime was called vagrancy. Vagrancy was the offense of a person not being able to prove at a given moment that he or she is employed. This crime was only aimed toward the black population at a time when there was massive unemployment among **ALL southern men.** Imagine that.

With this I've learned that the Police, provincial judges, local mayors, and justices of the peace- often white business owners who relied on the forced labor, were handing down the sentences of guilt.

Nothing has changed these made-up crimes against the blacks are still happening. As a matter of fact, the system was built to keep you committing crimes and to keep especially the black man down. I will explain this later.

Now, during slavery there was a group of white men called the Patrollers. Their job was to hunt and catch the runaway slaves. Any slaves caught not having a pass to travel often fell into their hands. The Patrollers, were allowed, to beat and even kill the slaves. This group still exists also under a new name called the Police. As back then they are still allowed to beat and kill the people of color without and reprimands.

When slavery supposed to have ended the poor Irish white men who were the Patrollers were upset because that was how they made a living. The higher whites told them not to worry they could become police and police the colored people. They would make sure that they kept the blacks impoverished therefore, forcing them into the life of crime. This system still exists today. Once, my people wake up and realize what is being done to them they will understand that slavery still exist and we're are under attack, the Bible calls it Spiritual Warfare.

To be honest, I had no clue that these things were happening. All I knew was that my people were suffering all over the world, and I noticed that we were also the most hated race of people on this planet. Coming into the truth the MOSTHIGH began to reveal to me just how bad it was. Now I'm going to try and show you.

Many of us know some of the atrocities that the slaves went through during slavery. During my research, I began to find out even more evil things that was done to our people. Some of those things that was done I couldn't believe that a human could do that to another human being. Some, examples are the human zoos, (featuring the negroes, and the Hispanics), alligator babies (the using of black babies for alligator bait), and sex farms. Used to breed more slaves. And many, many more.

Imagine being told that you were free, but then because of some law the rulers(oppressors) made up sent you right back into slavery. This slavery was just a cruel as the first, sometimes much worse and there was nothing that you or your family could do about it. This was also one of the fear by night and by day that Israel was prophesied to by Moses that would happen to them if they did not walk in the Most high's laws, and statutes. Many of us have this same fear today. It's not as horrible as it was back then, but admit it when you see a cop behind you what are your thoughts. I know because I have the same thoughts. Sad but true.

This slavery was horrible especially in a mine called Slope No. 12. (Pratt Mines) located on the edge of Birmingham. The slaves there were chained at night and were required to spend long as they were awake digging and loading coal. If they didn't get the amount that they were supposed to get they were whipped and or physically tortured. Not to mention being subjugated to the sexual intentions of the other miners. Just being a child, suffering this was horrible, yet along any human beings.

The Black woman was not exempt from the horrifying circumstance of being enslaved again. fed, and when they were fed it was in an inhumane way. Records showed that black women were stripped naked and whipped, hundreds of men starved, chained, and beaten, the slaves were lice-ridden and barely clothed.

In this slavery as the first slavery the slaves were worked to death then thrown into shallow graves, some of the corpse were put into ovens, or coal blasters. Great suffering that many don't know about. This is just some of the hidden history in America's slave era.

Many of us don't know that we are still in slavery to this day. America has never included the so-called African-American in their Constitution. They gave us the illusion that we were free. The country has and always will defend white Supremacy. Being black, you had, and still need to assimilate into the white society to even get treated as closely as an equal. All my life I have noticed the pride of the Edomite always being talked down to as if I couldn't understand what they were saying to me. I've seen the dirty looks, shaking of the head as if I was a pitiful case. Now, being fully awoke I understand why this was and still is happening.

These things are all in Deuteronomy 28 verses 15 through 68. There is no denying that we are still being mistreated, afflicted, and oppressed still to this day.

What many of us in the United States didn't know is that the 13th Amendment clearly states that though slavery is abolished except under punishment of a crime. This is what allowed America to still have slavery today. And I'm going to show you that they still use the 13th amendment to keep us enslaved.

I was led to a video on Netflix called 13th a documentary on the new slavery in America. I had no clue that existed. But, when the Most High uncovers what is hidden as he said he would do in the book of Obadiah, that is exactly what he meant. I am not the only one things to. Many of the awakened has also been shown these things. he revealed these

Isaiah 42:22 But this is a people robbed and spoiled; they are all of them snared in holes, and they are hid in prison houses; they are for a prey, and none delivereth; for a spoil, and none saith, Restore.

This scripture tells you that Israel are at the bottom suffering, and hid in prison houses, then he tells us there will be no deliverance from any man. So, we need to stop thinking that we will be getting reparations. It's not going to happen. He will be the only one to deliver us. It's going to be a repeat of him delivering the children of Israel from Egypt. This in the Bible is referred to as the greater Exodus, that all who are living shall see.

The 13th Amendment loop whole was immediately exploited, since 4 million blacks whom were formerly property were then free. America was used to having to pay their workers. They renamed a new slavery. Every time their oppressive systems gets outlawed they redesign it. So, to tell the truth slavery never left it's just hidden. Our oppressors have very craftily kept us in slavery, and at the same time made look like we are free.

Slavery, Convict Leasing, Jim Crow & Black Codes, and now Mass Incarceration & The New Jim Crow. These are all of the oppressive systems that we've been through as a nation to keep us down and in control. Let's not forget the terror also that the Blacks were also subjugated to. The lynchings, and forced to move out of their homes. Which these also has never left. Now it's the police killing us and the state taking your homes.

Watching the documentary 13th showed me that slavery never ended for us. It also showed me that we are still not considered as humans. (1960's Marched with sign stating that they were a Man, 2016 still marching with signs on their shirts stating that they are a Man.) The Constitution never meant to include us. Therefore, showing me that the Bible is absolutely correct when it shows me that our captivity is not over, and we are still in the land of our enemies. Many of my people still haven't found this out yet. But, the Most High keeps trying to show them. He's been trying to show them through the media. The media keep showing us our people dying by the hands of the Police.

According to the documentary America is home to only 5% of the total world population, but house 25% of the world's prisoners.

United States Prison Populations from 1972 until now:

300,000 in 1972

513,900 in 1980

759,000 in 1985

1,179,200 in 1990

2,300,000 present and still growing.

The Mass Incarceration ere began in 1970 with President Nixon declaring war on drugs, even though he was declaring war of the Black community seeing that there was no drug crisis. The crisis was that the blacks were rising tired of being mistreated. This war was more about throwing blacks in jail.

The modern day, war on drugs was declared by Ronald Regan in 1982. Still, lying about the drug problem. This strategy helped him to get elected. Ronald's campaign strategist, Lee Atwater, was caught on tape saying these words:

"You start out in 1954 by saying nigger, nigger, nigger. By 1968 you can't say nigger, that hurts you. It backfires. So, you say stuff like forced-bussing, state's rights and all that stuff. You're getting so abstract now. You're talking about cutting taxes and all of those things you're talking about are totally economic things… And the by-product of them is blacks get hurt more than whites."

Now, this is something my people don't have a clue about. We have been in a spiritual warfare since our ancestors step their foot on this soil, and throughout all of the other nations. Now, I'm going to give you scripture to show you that this is in the Bible, it's just that many of us didn't understand it until he us up and showed us. Then he brought us to the information such as the Documentary 13th, that proves the Bible right.

Micah 2:1 Woe to them that devise iniquity, and work evil on their beds! When the morning is light, they practice it, because it is in the power of their hand.

Bill Clinton/ Al Gore competed to be more tough on crime to get elected. Clinton did more damage to the Blacks than any other President. The Federal Crime Bill of 1994 introduced by Clinton increased funding to States to build more prisons, and add 100,000 Police to the streets. Mandatory sentencing, and the 3 strikes law came from this bill. Therefore, more black males in history were incarcerated.

Edom has striped the blacks of their leaders, killed, and framed our people. They have left us destroyed and vulnerable, so they will do to you what they will. With that in mind you need to understand that the main people of color that has been targeted are the leaders. I've found out that many of our business men, educated men are the main people that are being locked up. Many, if not all, are innocent. So, you high and mighty ones are not exempt from this. This can happen to you also.

In my research I found out about ALEC it stands for American Legislative Exchange Council. It is a political lobbying group that write laws and give them to the Republicans. Stand Your Ground law was written by ALEC. ALEC is a private club whose members are Politicians and Corporations. Corporations have been writing laws for years through ALEC. Why, because every one of ALEC'S Bills benefit one of its corporate funder. Some of the corporations linked to ALEC include: Exxon Mobil, Direct TV, Time Warner Cable, Altria, Pfizer, *Walmart, State Farm, PhRMA, Comcast, Du Pont, FedEx, KOCH Industries Inc., Wells Fargo, Google, Johnson-Johnson, Visa, Coca-Cola, Kraft, Bank of America, Ebay, American Bail Coalition, P&G, Ford, NRA, Shell, Facebook, GM, Wendy's, Sprint, Tobaco Indusrty, AT&T, Verizon, CCA (Corrections Corporations of America).

CCA (Corrections Corporations of America) Build, own, and manage prisons. CCA were the first private prison corporation in the United States. Now there are more private own Prisons. Which require to keep the prisons filled even if there were no crimes committing the crime.

There are also private owned detention centers which came about from the ALEC BILL SB1070. The most hurt were the immigrants in Arizona.

The most hurt in our prison systems are the Israelites. Many of them who don't know who they are.

The Most High had me doing this research to find out that we are not free and won't be free until he comes back and redeem us. The Christian church has no idea what redeem means according to the Bible.

Redeemed: To be bought back buy your kinsman.

John 4:22 Ye worship ye know not what; we know what we worship: for salvation is of the Jews.

If you are not keeping the laws as was commanded then you worship that which you don't know. You are worshiping Satan thinking that you are worshiping the God of Abraham, Isaac, and Jacob.

Proverbs 14:12 There is a way which seemeth right unto a man, but the end thereof are the ways of death.

For the devil deceived the whole world. How by giving the world a different doctrine. Through Christianity they teach that the laws are done away with. The Bible destroys all of the Christian lies. Now, I'm going to show you who how Satan deceived the world using the scriptures. And many of the people will stay deceived as prophesied in Thessalonians.

2 Thessalonians 2:10 And with all deceivableness of unrightousness in them that perish; because they received not the love of truth, that they might be saved.

2 Thessalonians 2:11 And for this cause Yah shall send them strong delusion, that they should believe a lie:

2 Thessalonians 2:12 That they all might be damned who believed not the truth, but had pleasure in unrightousness.(not keeping the laws).

CHAPTER 3 THE BIG DECEPTION

I'm going to show you how the great deception came in and who the people are that are responsible for this great deception. Christianity for the most part came in through the Edomite nation. Edom has always been in paganism. Esau has never kept the laws, or showed an interest in pleasing the Most High. Instead of learning how to live right from his grandfather Shem, he wanted to go hunting.

Malachi 1:4 Whereas Edom saith, We are impoverished, but we will return and build the desolate places; thus saith Yah of hosts, they shall build, but I will throw down; and they shall call them, The border of wickedness, and, The people against whom Yah hath indignation forever.

In that verse it tells you about the fall of Rome in 193 A.D. Then it tells you that they will rebuild again this is talking about the Renaissance, (1453) which is the rebirth of the white man in power. But from there he will begin to destroy their kingdom until the final throw down of their kingdom as stated in **Isaiah 66: 15.**

Isaiah 66:15 For, behold, Yah will come with fire, and with his chariots like a whirlwind, to render his anger with fury, and his rebuke with flames of fire.

Isaiah 66:16 For by fire and by his sword will Yah plead with all flesh: and the slain of Yah shall be many.

Then the last sentence in **Malachi 1:4** lets us know Edom is the wicked that the Bible speaks of. When he called them the border of wickedness, he was saying that they are the beginning and ending of wickedness. Therefore, letting us know that this is the man of sin. It is not one man but a nation of people, the Edomites.

According, to history and still to this day the Edomites as a nation has always used the Eagle as it's symbol beginning with Rome, Greece, France, Spain, Germany, Russia, Britain, and America. In the Bible 99.9% of the time the eagle is mentioned it is in a bad way. According, to the Bible these eagle nations are being used to oppress Israel and all the other nations. This is their sole purpose of being. He created them for destruction. To show himself to the world. He did this also with the Pharaoh of Egypt which was also a world power who had Israel enslaved and also used the Eagle as their symbol. To prove this with scripture:

Deuteronomy 28:49 Yah shall bring a nation against thee from far, from the end of the earth, as swift as the eagle flieth; a nation whose tongue thou shalt not understand;

II Esdras 14:17 For the weaker the world becomes through old age, the more shall evils be increased upon its inhabitants.

II Esdras 14:18 Truth shall go further away, and falsehood shall come near. For the eagle that you saw in the vision is already hurrying to come.

In that verse it lets you know that when the kingdom of the Eagle comes truth will not be on earth. For he will come deceiving many with his lies. I will prove this with more scriptures. Now, Christianity teaches that there is going to arise a one man who will be the Devils son, with power deceiving many by acting as if he is Christ. This is their Anti-Christ belief. During this time, he will cause many to get the mark of the beast (chip in right hand or forehead). They believe this period to be the great tribulation in which those who are saved will escape through the rapture. Believing that while tribulation for the world is going on they will be in heaven having supper and getting their rewards for being faithful. This proves that they have no understanding of what they read in the Bible. I'm going to break these scriptures down and give you the true meaning of these verses. Christianity also believes that all people can be saved and rule in the kingdom. I'm sorry to say that that is not in the Bible. Most of this is kind of right, but the Anti-Christ is already here and has already deceived the world. Many people already have the mark and don't realize it. The mark is not a chip in your forehead or right hand. It is not keeping the commandments or sin. When you set God's laws down a keep man's traditions and his policies or democracies you have the mark.

First, of all, according, to the Bible the Anti-Christ is a nation of people (Edomites). The tribulation period is for one people. Those people are Israel, have you ever read the time of tribulation called Jacob's Trouble? This tribulation is when they are in their worst captivity (Slavery in all other nations.) Which is also the meaning of the great falling away. During this time they would lose their heritage, culture, Identity, power, images, and all. Scripture that reveals this is **Hosea 3:4**

Hosea 3:4 For the children of Israel shall abide many without a king, and without a prince, and without a sacrifice, and without an image, and without an ephod, and without teraphim:

They will also dwell in a strange land that they nor their fathers had known meaning the western hemisphere. Meaning they will be in the Americas, Europe, Spain, Netherlands, they will be in every nation throughout the four corners of the earth getting treated bad for 400 years. At the end of the 400 years Christ will come back and redeem them from their oppressors, then they shall rule over their oppressors. Meaning, there will be slavery in the new kingdom. All nations that enslaved Israel shall go into captivity. And this is all in your Bible, but Christianity doesn't teach this, Why? Because Christianity is the main religion of the Anti-Christ. This is one of the ways he deceived the Whole World. Christianity and Democracy is the same thing and they are both the white man's philosophy. Scripture proof:

Deuteronomy 30:7 And YAH UAH thy ALL MIGHTY will put all these curses upon thine enemies, and on them that hate thee, which persecuted thee.

Obadiah 1:15 For the day of the Yah is near upon all the heathen: as thou hast done, it shall be done unto thee: thy reward shall return upon thine own head.

Amos 9:12 That they may possess the remnant of Edom, and of all the heathen, which are called by my name, saith Yah that doeth this.

2 Thessalonians 1:6 Seeing it is a righteous thing with Yah to recompense tribulation to them that trouble you.

Meaning no one escapes tribulation, the tribulation is the curse of **Deuteronomy 28: 15-68.** Israel is still in their tribulation but it is almost over. Do you remember the scripture that Judgment starts at God's house, well many of the Christians got the wrong interpretation. The judgment that the MOST HIGH was talking about is tribulation which is the curse of **Deuteronomy 28:15-68.** Many people don't know Yah's judgements. Yah's Judgment is slavery, and all that comes with it.

I know that this is a hard pill to swallow, many of us was raised to believe that God loves everybody and that he is all love. That also shows that no one is reading or understanding their Bible's. The Most High is also a man of war, and judgement. And he is not happy with the people. He is angry with the people especially Edom.

Romans 9:13 As it is written, Jacob have I loved, but Esau have I hated.

Romans 9:22 What if Yah, willing to show his wrath, and to make his power known, endured with much longsuffering the vessels of wrath fitted to destruction:

Those scripture shows you that he hates the Edomites, and that they were made for destruction to show his power. Does this sound familiar? Do you remember the Pharaoh of Egypt whom Yah raised to show his power which was also fitted for destruction. Just like Egypt the Edomites are so powerful that only God can bring them down.

II Esdras 12:24 And of those that dwell therein, with much oppression, above all those that were before them: therefore are they called the heads of the eagle.

II Esdras 12:25 For these are they that shall accomplish his wickedness, and that shall finish his last end.

Job 9:24 The earth is giving into the hand of the wicked: he covereth the faces of the judges thereof, if not where, and who is he?

How did the wicked cover the faces of the Judges, meaning Christ and his people the prophets and his people Israel, **I Maccabees** tells you.
I Maccabees 3:48 And laid open the book of the law, wherein the heathen had sought to paint the likeness of their images.

If you pay attention you should notice in these Bibles that have pictures in them portraying the Apostles look more like Roman God's with short robes, and half of their chest covered. Whereas the Bible told you that they wore long robes and britches and were fully covered.

Now to show you more proof of your false images created by the white man.

Wisdom of Solomon 14:15 For a father afflicted with untimely mourning, when he hath made an image of his child soon taken away, now honored him as a god, which was then a dead man, and delivered to those that were under him ceremonies and sacrifices.

Wisdom of Solomon 14:16 Thus in process of time an ungodly custom grown strong was kept as a law, and graven images were worshipped by the commandment of kings.

Wisdom of Solomon 14:17 Whom men could now as but at honor in presence, because they dwelt far off, they took the counterfeit of his visage from far, and made an express image of a king whom they honored, to the end that by this their forwardness they might flatter him that was absent, as if he were present.

Wisdom of Solomon 14:20 And so the multitude, allured by the grace of the work, took him for a god, which a little before was but honored as a man.

Wisdom of Solomon 12:21 And this was an occasion to deceive the world: for men, serving either calamity or tyranny, did ascribe unto stones and stocks the incommunicable name.

These verses tell you about the Christian Image of Christ given to you by the White man (Edom) which his real name while he was alive was Ceasre Biorge. He was the sixth pope's son. His lover Leanordo Divince painted him to be the image of Christ. This is your renaissance image. Which also explains why Christianity has an effeminate spirit in it. This is also the image of the beast that the Bible speaks of.

Have you noticed that the white man has done nothing but killed, stole, and destroy many nations? He has conquered lands then renamed them after his own name. This is another way the world has been deceived. No one knows who they are according to the Bible. In Genesis the Most High gave a name to all nations by their forefathers. It also gives you the characteristics of the main two nations that play a big part in prophecies. Those Nations are the Israelites, and the Edomites. Now, I'm going to show you that it was prophesied how Esau would get his lands and come into power. In **Genesis.**

Genesis 27:39 And Isaac his father answered and said unto him, Behold thy dwelling shall be the fatness of the earth, and the dew of the heaven from above (meaning the best places all over the earth);

Genesis 27:40 And by thy sword shalt thy live, (how they got their land)

According, to history we know this is true. How did they get the Americas, Africa, Europe, and so on? Do you know that according to the Bible, United States of America (aka Babylon the Great) is still killing, robbing the other nations, and destroying their nations to this very day? Which will help to start WWIII, nuclear destruction as the Bible said would happen. Do you now that we are very close to the war starting? I will prove this with scriptures.

Now to give you the beginning of the Anti-Christ. Starting with the scripture. Beginning with the Greeks (Antiochus Epiphanes).

1 Maccabees 1:41 Moreover king Antiochus wrote to his whole kingdom, that all should be one people.

1 Maccabees 1:42 And every one should leave his laws: so all the heathen agreed according to the commandment of the king.

1 Maccabees 1:43 Yea, many also of the Israelites consented to his religion, (democracy all one people; familiar??? America) and sacrificed unto idols, and profaned the Sabbath.

Just like today like for instance the Muslims have their own culture and the way they dress, but for some reason when they get over here in America, they slowly began to change dropping their laws and looking more like Edom. The woman aren't in their dresses and head coverings any more. Therefore, they have consulted to Edom's religion. The same with us in slavery we have lost all of our customs and now we are as the heathen, consulting to his religion. The Chinese also dress like the Europeans. All who does business with America are looking like America.

1 Maccabees 1:44 For the king had sent letters by messengers unto Jerusalem and the cities of Judah, that they should follow the strange laws of the land,

1 Maccabees 1:45 And forbid burnt offerings, and sacrifice, and drink offerings, in the temple; and that they should profane the Sabbaths and festival days;

1 Maccabees 1:46 And pollute the sanctuary and holy people:

1 Maccabees 1:49 To the end they might forget the law, and change all the ordinances.

1 Maccabees 1:54 Now the fifteenth day of the month Casleu, in the hundred forty and fifth year, they set up the abomination of desolation upon the alter, and builded idol altars throughout the cities of Judah on every side; (hum? Another thing Christians waiting for has already happened.)

1 Maccabees 1:56 And when they had rent in pieces the books of the law (aka Bible) which they found, they burnt them with fire. (Another event that already happened)

1 Maccabees 1:57 And wheresoever was found with any the book of the testament, or if any to the law, the king's commandment was, that they should be put to death.

In those verses it shows you the tribulation of the Israelites. Which many people are still waiting for today. If people would just research they will find that everything that they are waiting for to happen has already happened. While they are waiting for those things to happen they are missing out on the last couple of prophecies that are being fulfilled today.

In the scriptures it tells us that the antichrist will think to change times and laws. This is something that the Christians are also still waiting for today not realizing that this also was already done. Scripture proof:

Genesis 1:4 And Yah saw the light, that it was good: and Yah divided the light from the darkness.

Genesis 1:5 And Yah called the light Day, and the darkness he called Night. And the evening and the and the morning were the first day.

Genesis 1:8 And Yah called the firmament Heaven. And the evening and the morning were the second day.

Genesis 1:13 And the evening and the morning were the third day.

Genesis 1:19 And the evening and the morning were the fourth day.

Genesis 1:23 And the evening and the morning were the fifth day.

Genesis 1: 31 And the evening and the morning were the sixth day.

According, to the Bible our days are supposed to be from sundown to sundown. So, can anyone tell me why our days now begin at Midnight. The antichrist already changed this. Another thing that was changed was the beginning of the year. According, to the Bible the year begins in Spring, but man tells us it begins in the dead of the winter. Common sense should tell us that the year begins with everything new such as spring. Yes, we have all been duped. Now, just remember. "The devil deceiveth the whole world." Are you convinced yet? There's more. The law of the Sabbath has also been change to Sunday, which the MOST HIGH gave no one authority, to do that. Yes, they give you some story that Christ died on a Friday and rose on a Sunday so therefore worship on Sunday. This story is unsearchable in the scriptures. As a matter of fact it is a lie.

Daniel 9:27 And he shall confirm the covenant with many for one week: and in the midst of the week he shall cause the sacrifice and the oblation to cease, and for the overspreading of abominations he shall make it desolate, even until the consummation, and that determined shall be poured upon the desolate.

Matthew 28:1 In the end of the sabbath, as it began to dawn towards the first day of the week (the first day is Sunday), came Mary Magdalene and the other Mary to see the sepulcher. (And we know the rest, the Angle told them that he was already risen.) meaning he had already risen on the Sabbath.

Those two scriptures prove that he died on a Wednesday and rose on the Sabbath. Daniel 9 also kills the teaching that he nailed the laws to the cross. It tells us that he did away with the that animal sacrifice. Therefore, ours sins can be covered by his blood but the grace we're under is giving you time to repent from your sins and come back to the father and keep his laws. Now, that false teaching which came from the enemy your oppressor, has gotten many people blinded and headed for destruction. Proof of this is in **II Esdras:**

II Esdras 9:19 For then everyone obeyed: but now the manners of them which are created in world that is made are corrupted by a perpetual seed, and by a law which is unsearchable rid themselves.

For instance, the sabbath being change to Sunday because he died of a Friday and rose on a Sunday, is no where in the scriptures. You will be destroyed for not keeping his commandments. You can go around quoting **John 3:16** all you want but just believing in Christ is not going to save you for like the scriptures tells you that Satan believes in Christ also, but he won't be saved. For faith without works is dead. The works in that scripture is talking about the laws, statutes, and commandments.

So, by keeping these Christian lies, which is the religion of Edom, aka the son of perdition, aka, the Anti-Christ, will get you, Israel eternal condemnation. The laws were only given to you and this is your last chance to get it right. Or you will burn with Babylon. Remember, the Most High knows everything and has declared everything in the Bible from the Beginning to the Ending. Which, he tells us that 2/3's of his people won't listen and will be destroyed. I pray that you begin to dig in to history and research. The information is there, pray for truth and he will guide you then your eyes too will be open and you'll begin to see that you've been living a lie your whole life.

Printed in the United States
By Bookmasters